Planet Omar

Adapted by Asif Khan

Based on the novel by Zanib Mian

methuen | drama
LONDON • NEW YORK • OXFORD • NEW DELHI • SYDNEY

METHUEN DRAMA
Bloomsbury Publishing Plc, 50 Bedford Square, London, WC1B 3DP, UK
Bloomsbury Publishing Inc, 1359 Broadway, New York, NY 10018, USA
Bloomsbury Publishing Ireland, 29 Earlsfort Terrace, Dublin 2, D02 AY28, Ireland

BLOOMSBURY, METHUEN DRAMA and the Methuen Drama logo are trademarks of Bloomsbury Publishing Plc

First published in Great Britain 2026

Cover design and photography by FEAST

A catalogue record for this book is available from the British Library.

A catalog record for this book is available from the Library of Congress.

ISBN: PB: 978-1-3506-4204-1
ePDF: 978-1-3506-4205-8
eBook: 978-1-3506-4206-5

Series: Modern Plays

Typeset by Westchester Publishing Services

For product safety related questions contact productsafety@bloomsbury.com.

To find out more about our authors and books visit www.bloomsbury.com and sign up for our newsletters.

Planet Omar

Adapted by Asif Khan

Planet Omar

This adaptation of *Planet Omar* was commissioned by Leeds Playhouse.

Planet Omar is a production by Leeds Playhouse, in association with the Unicorn Theatre and Birmingham Repertory Theatre.

It was first presented at Leeds Playhouse in April 2026. The cast and creative team who made the show were:

Cast

Omar	**Justin Kendal-Sadiq**
Mum	**Aizah Khan**
Dad	**Umar Butt**
Daniel/Maryam	**Emaan Durrani**
Charlie/Daniel's Mum	**Izzy Coward**
Mrs Rodgers/ Mrs Hutchinson	**Joanna Holden**

Creative Team

Adaptor	**Asif Khan**
Director	**Sameena Hussain**
Set, Costume & Puppet Designer and Puppet Director	**Nikki Charlesworth**
Lighting Designer	**Sam Osborne**
Sound Designer & Composer	**Helen Skiera**
Movement Director & Voice Coach	**Zoe Katsilerou**
Fight Director	**Kenan Ali**
Associate Lighting Designer	**Ryan Dunnett**
Casting Director	**Lucy Casson CDG**

Production

Producer	**Zoe Bailey**
Production Manager	**Sophie Slater**
Project Producer	**Javairya Khan**
Company Stage Manager (Leeds)	**Steve Cressy**
Stage Manager (Leeds)	**Michelle Booth**
Company Stage Manager (Unicorn & Birmingham)	**Aiman Bandali**
Deputy Stage Manager	**Amy Duckworth**
Assistant Stage Manager	**Sofie Mirza**
Costume Supervisor	**Claire Powell**
Props Supervisor	**Nathan Rose**
WHAM Supervisor	**Lucy Skeldon**
Wardrobe & WHAM Manager	**Casan Fiore**

Costume, Set, Props & Puppets made by Leeds Playhouse

Cast

UMAR BUTT Dad

Umar is an actor, writer, director, theatre maker and a Tees Valley Artist of the year 2025. He speaks Urdu, Punjabi and English, and makes relevant and representative work for communities specifically but not limited to those of the Global Majority.

Recent acting credits: *A Teaspoon of Shampoo* (Theatre in the Mill); *The Jungle Book* (Theatre by the Lake); *Macbeth* (Proteus Theatre Company); *My Name Is...* (Tamasha Theatre Company); *Welcome to the Jungle* (ARC Stockton); *Bird in the Window*; *Alex & Eliza* (national tour); *What Is Love?* (ARC Stockton); *Taggart* (ITV); *Big Sky* (BBC Radio 4).

IZZY COWARD Charlie/Daniel's Mum

Izzy is a Lancastrian actor based in Manchester. They trained at Bristol Old Vic Theatre School, graduating in 2020.

Stage credits include: *Macbeth* (Grange Theatre); *Three Minute Monologues* (Middle Child Theatre); Celia in *As You Like It* (Northern Broadsides); She/Her/She/Mother & Other in *Qweershorts* (Queerdog Theatre); Francesca in *In a Room with Gavin & Francesca* (National Theatre Education); two appearances in *OutStageUs* (Hive North/Hope Mill Theatre 2021/2022); Naomi in *Home Girl* (Derby Theatre); Loz in *Decades 1980s: Nicer Than Orange Squash* (Leeds Playhouse).

Short film credits include: Florence in *Uncool* (BFI/Little Stitch Productions); Ash in *Six Minutes*; Jessie in *Cat's Cradle* (Knock and Nash); Claire in *Two Steps Forward* (038 Films); and Rose in *Rose* (Izzy Pye).

They are thrilled to be making their return to Leeds Playhouse.

EMAAN DURRANI Daniel/Maryam

Emaan graduated from Bristol Old Vic Theatre School in 2025. This is her professional stage debut.

Credits whilst training include Elizabeth Watson in *The Watsons* and Helen Ludlow in *The Welkin*.

Other work includes *Jealous People Are Ugly People* (BBC).

JOANNA HOLDEN Mrs Rodgers/Mrs Hutchinson

Joanna has worked for The London Performance Studio, Hull Truck, Bolton Octogon, Stephen Joseph Theatre, Polka, Told by an Idiot, Clowns without Borders, Bamboozle Theatre, Creation Theatre, Lyceum Edinburgh, Bristol Old Vic, York Theatre Royal, The British Library, Manchester Royal Exchange, Live Theatre, Northern Stage, Svenska Theatre, Soho Theatre, Keswick Theatre, Bush Theatre, The Royal Court, Bolton Octagon, Royal National Theatre, Sheffield Crucible, Perth Rep, The Gate, The Tricycle, The Gilded Balloon, Vamos, Kneehigh, Cirque du Soleil, Cartoon de Salvo, Royal Shakespeare Company and The Ding Foundation.

JUSTIN KENDAL-SADIQ Omar

Justin graduated from the Royal Central School of Speech & Drama with an MA Acting for Screen in 2024.

He is a Northern actor whose work spans television, video games, theatre, short films and commercials. He is a proud alumnus of David Johnson Drama.

He has completed recording for two major AAA video games series to be released in 2026 and is also known for his series-regular role as Andy Stevens on CBBC's BAFTA Award-winning *Secret Life of Boys*.

AIZAH KHAN Mum

Aizah is a Midlands-based actor of Pakistani heritage. She is a passionate character artist who loves to explore new ways of telling stories. With experience across stage, screen, circus, puppeteering, voice and movement she is a versatile performer always ready to test the limits of her toolbox.

Theatre and puppetry includes *WILD* (UK tour); *Life of Pi* (UK and international tour); *Bradford Rise* (City of Culture); *The Many Lives of PET#1* (Stans Cafe); *Silence* (European tour); *Come Bowl with Me* (Talking Birds); *Coventry Moves* (City of Culture); *A Christmas Carol* (Albany Theatre); *Milesians – The Coming of the Gaels*; *A Winter's Tale* (Poland).

Television includes *Phoenix Rise* (BBC); *I Told My Mum I Was Going on an RE Trip*; *Performance Live*.

Commercial and voiceover campaigns for Ladbrokes, Kellogg's, Chilly's, Woven Ink, Resume Foundation.

Circus includes *Around the World in 80 days* (Rogueplay); *Freaks and Beasts* (Rebel Productions); *Christmas of Dreams.*

Creative Team

ASIF KHAN Adaptor

Asif's debut play *Combustion* toured the UK in 2017 and was nominated for OffWestEnd's Best New Play Award and Best Writer in the Stage Debut Awards. It also Won Best Production at the Eastern Eye Arts, Culture and Theatre Awards (2018) and at the Asian Media Awards (2017). As part of the BBC Comedy Room in 2017, he was named on the BBC New Talent Hotlist (2017). In 2018, Asif won the Channel 4 Playwrights' Scheme Award. In 2019, his play *Imaam Imraan* was produced by the National Youth Theatre, playing at the Bradford Literary Festival. His children's play *Jabala and the Jinn* was first live-streamed (during lockdown) from Belgrade Theatre (Coventry), before going on a UK tour in 2022. For this play, Asif won Best Script Writer at the Eastern Eye Arts, Culture and Theatre Awards 2022. In 2025, his play *Sisters 360*, inspired by real-life skateboarding siblings, premiered at Polka Theatre, before transferring to Leeds Playhouse and Bradford City of Culture. It is set to go on an extensive UK tour in 2026.

Asif trained as an actor at RADA and works regularly on stage, screen and radio.

Find out more at: www.theasifkhan.com.

SAMEENA HUSSAIN Director

Sameena is a freelance theatre director and facilitator based in West Yorkshire. She was Associate Director at Leeds Playhouse 2021–5 and has worked with Hull Truck Theatre, Opera North, Kiln Theatre, Lawrence Batley Theatre, RSC and Soho Theatre.

Sameena's work is rooted in community and connection. Since she started her career she's been on a mission to remove barriers (both invisible and visible) preventing people from engaging with theatre and her projects have included everything from heritage projects and directing intergenerational performances, to creating and delivering artist development programmes and co-leading anti-racist strategies in institutions.

Sameena is passionate about making theatre a safe and brave space, enabling dialogue and connection and was recently Community Co-Director for RISE the opening event of Bradford City of Culture.

Recent director credits include: *Peanut Butter and Blueberries* (Kiln Theatre); *Romeo and Juliet* (Leeds Conservatoire); *A Christmas Carol* (Hull Truck Theatre); *I Wanna Be Yours*, *Decades* (Leeds Playhouse); *Our White Skoda Octavia* (Eastern Angels); *La Voix Humaine* (Opera North & Leeds Playhouse)

Associate director credits include: *A Christmas Carol*, *Dr Korczak's Example*, *Night Before Christmas*, *There Are No Beginnings*, *Europe*, *Road* (Leeds Playhouse); *Henry V* (Lawrence Batley Theatre)

NIKKI CHARLESWORTH Set, Costume & Puppet Designer and Puppet Director

Nikki is a theatre designer and maker, puppet designer and puppeteer. She trained at Nottingham Trent University, graduating in 2017.

In her professional life she has worked at the forefront of disabled-led theatre making, contributing to ground-breaking new work. Her work as a designer has visited both theatres and unconventional spaces across the UK and internationally.

Recent/current collaborations include: Diverse City, Buxton Opera House, 1623 Theatre Company, LipService Theatre and OperaUpClose. Nikki also creates new work as designer and director under Nikki Charlesworth Productions and has toured nationally and internationally. Her work is unique in its nurturing focus on puppetry, health and disability for young audiences. Shows include: *What Happened to You?* and *The Luckiest Girl Alive*.

SAM OSBORNE Lighting Designer

Sam is a freelance lighting designer based in Nottingham and works around the UK as a lighting designer, and internationally as an associate and programmer.

Credits as lighting designer: *The Little Mermaid* (Nottingham Playhouse); *The Secret Garden* (BigLittle Theatre); *The Ugly Duckling* (Nottingham Playhouse); *The Winter's Tale* (1623); *Barbara* (Mark Croasdale); *Gnaw* (Daniel McVey); *Kennington Loop* (Loudest Laugh); *Choose Your Fighter* (Votive Theatre).

As associate lighting designer: *A Christmas Carol* (Leeds Playhouse); *The Wild Cards* (Sisco Ents); *Animal Farm* (Theatre Royal Stratford East/Leeds Playhouse); *Future Fest* (Abandoman); *The Lost Spells* (Goblin/Watford Palace); *A Christmas Carol* (Hull Truck); *Stranger Sings!* (The Vaults); THEM (Body Politic).

Credits as lighting programmer: *A Christmas Carol* (Leeds Playhouse); *Animal Farm* (TRSE); *Uncanny* (Tilted Sessions); *Macplebs* (The Raymondos); *Romeo and Juliet* (Lakeside Arts); *Take Care* (Lakeside Arts); *THEM* (Body Politic).

HELEN SKIERA Sound Designer & Composer

Credits as sound designer: *Porn Play* (Royal Court Theatre); *Juniper Blood* (Donmar Warehouse); *Toto Kerblammo!* (Unicorn Theatre); *Peanut Butter and Blueberries* (The Kiln); *Mind Mangler: Member of the Tragic Circle* (Mischief/Apollo Theatre/UK tour/Virgin Voyages); *F**ked Up Bedtime Stories Series 2* (English Touring Theatre); *Cinderella*, *Red Riding Hood* (Theatre Royal Stratford East); *Not: Lady Chatterley's Lover* (Happy Idiot Productions/UK tour); *The Long Song* (Chichester Festival Theatre); *A Christmas Carol* (Bristol Old Vic); *The Lovely Bones* (Birmingham REP/UK tour); *Out of Water* (Orange Tree); *Silence* (Mercury); *Here I Belong* (Pentabus); *This Is Not for You* (Graeae GDIF/SIRF); *Instructions for Correct Assembly*, *Bodies* (Royal Court); *Imber: You Walk Through*, *Betrayal*, *Echo's End*, *The Magna Carta Plays* (Salisbury Playhouse).

As associate: *Lander 23* (Punchdrunk); *Viola's Room* (Punchdrunk); *The Dark Is Rising* (BBC/Complicite audio drama); *The Encounter* (Complicité); *East is East* (Birmingham REP/Chichester Festival Theatre); *Touching The Void* (Duke of York's); *Barbershop Chronicles* (National Theatre); *Cat on a Hot Tin Roof* (Young Vic/Apollo Theatre).

ZOE KATSILEROU Movement Director & Voice Coach

Zoe is a movement director, choreographer and performer working across theatre and dance. She specialises in working with actors, supporting them to develop physical presence, emotional clarity, and a strong connection between voice and movement.

Zoe has worked as a movement director across theatre, community-led performance and film.

Her recent credits include Stand and Be Counted Theatre's touring production *Ripples* and work with Coventry City of Sanctuary, alongside short films and a range of independent theatre productions across the UK. She is particularly passionate about collaborative processes that place the body at the heart of narrative and social storytelling.

She is the founder and artistic director of MOV Dance Theatre, a company creating bold dance-theatre that amplifies underrepresented voices. Her recent work includes *Voices*, an interdisciplinary performance developed with Roma communities that celebrates heritage, identity and resilience through movement and music.

Zoe is also a Senior Lecturer at Leeds Beckett University, where she teaches movement for actors and directs bold, innovative performances with students across all years.

Zoe's movement direction is rooted in curiosity, musicality and the belief that the body carries unique stories that can transform the audience experience.

KENAN ALI Fight Director

Theatre includes: *Standing at the Sky's Edge* (National Theatre); *Accidental Death of an Anarchist, Guys and Dolls, Standing at the Sky's Edge, A Midsummer Night's Dream* (Sheffield Theatres); *Cat on a Hot Tin Roof*, *Betty!*, *Electric Rosary*, *A Doll's House*, *The Mountaintop*, *Queen Margaret*, *Death of a Salesman*, *The Producers*, *Mother Courage and Her Children*, *Wuthering Heights*, *Rockets and Blue Lights* (Royal Exchange, Manchester); *Oliver!*, *Charlie and the Chocolate Factory*, *Oliver Twist* (Leeds Playhouse); *One Man*, *Two Guvnors*, *Kes*, *Treasure Island* (Bolton Octagon); *Beauty and the Beast* (Stoke New Vic); *Romeo and Juliet*, *Peter Pan* (Hull Truck Theatre); *A Greasy Spoon* (Royal Court Liverpool), *Work It Out* (Home) *The Kaspar Hauser Experiment* (Animikii Theatre); *Treasure Island* (Stephen Joseph Theatre); *Mother of Him* (Park Theatre); *Lost Boys* (The Unity); *Romeo and Juliet* (Moving Stories); *The Jungle Book* (Derby Theatre); *The Bone Sparrow*, *Noughts & Crosses* (Pilot Theatre); *Aladdin* (The Broadway Theatre); *Peter Pan* (Pomegranate Theatre); *Beauty and the Beast*; *Dick Whittington* (Imagine Theatre); *Peter Pan* (The Lowry).

Television includes: *Coronation Street* (ITV); *STAD* (S4C).

Film includes: *Purgatory*, *Wait for Me, Blank*, *Soldiers of the Damned* (short films); *Happy Hour*, *The Wilds*, *Circuit*, *Rabbit Punch*.

RYAN DUNNETT Associate Lighting Designer

Ryan is a freelance associate lighting designer and lighting programmer. Having trained at Rose Bruford College, he graduated in creative lighting control. Based in London he has worked in venues across the UK and internationally including Germany, Spain and Japan.

Recent credits as an associate lighting designer include: *Friends: The Musical Parody* – UK tour (Mark Goucher); *Libera* – Japan tour; *Libera* – Montserrat, Spain.

Recent credits as a lighting programmer include: Carlos Acosta's *Nutcracker in Havana* – UK tour (Norwich Theatre Royal); *Midnight* (Sadler's Wells East); *Macbeth* (Chester Storyhouse); *Murder on the Orient Express – Germany tour* (Show Slot); *Robin Hood* – Cheltenham Everyman (Mark Goucher); *Midnight Cowboy* (Southwark Playhouse Elephant).

LUCY CASSON CDG Casting Director

Credits as casting director for Leeds Playhouse: *Small Island*, *A Christmas Carol*, *Animal Farm*, *Through It All Together*, *Macbeth*, *Lord of the Flies*, *Nine Night*, *I Wanna Be Yours*, *Say Yes to Tess*, *Decades and Dr Korczak's Example.*

Credits as casting director: *Lego Friends: Heartlake the Musical* (TV film); *Hamilton* (UK & Ireland tour); *Crime and Punishment* (Northern Broadsides); *A Knight's Tale* (Manchester Opera House); *101 Dalmatians: The Musical* (Eventim Apollo, UK & Ireland tour); *Club Nvrlnd* (Assembly Checkpoint); *Newsies* (Wembley Park Theatre); *Operation Epsilon*, *Straight White Men* (Southwark Playhouse); *Clybourne Park*, *Gently Down the Stream* (Park Theatre); *Who's Afraid of Virginia Woolf?* (Bristol Tobacco Factory); *Hedda Gabler* (Sherman Theatre); *Reasons to Stay Alive* (Sheffield Theatres/ETT); *The Merchant of Venice* (Stafford Shakespeare).

Credits as casting associate/assistant: *Upgraded* (Amazon Films); *The Bay S1* (ITV); *Murdered by My Father* (BBC); *Equus* (Stratford East/ETT); *An American in Paris* (West End); *A Midsummer Night's Dream* (RSC).

With huge thanks to all the teams at Leeds Playhouse, the Unicorn Theatre and Birmingham Repertory Theatre.

About Zanib Mian

Zanib Mian's books have featured on BBC's *CBeebies Bedtime Stories* and *The Guardian* for their contribution to diversity in children's literature. She was a World Book Day author in 2021, and her work has been translated into multiple languages. Zanib studied Molecular Cell Biology at University College London and went on to teach science in secondary schools before she made the decision to give up the career to create change within children's publishing. She felt that diverse characters from all minorities and backgrounds weren't being fully represented in books for young children. She launched Sweet Apple Publishers with a clear commitment to publishing inclusive books, many of which she has authored herself. *Planet Omar: Accidental Trouble Magnet* is a BookTrust '100 best children's books of the last 100 years'. The five-book *Planet Omar* series is published by Hachette Children's Group, along with Zanib's follow-up series, *Meet the Maliks*.

About Nasaya Mafaridik

Nasaya Mafaridik is the illustrator of *Planet Omar: Accidental Trouble Magnet* and is based in Indonesia. Self-taught, she has a passion for children's books and bright, colourful stationery. Nasaya can be found on Instagram: @synasaya

About Leeds Playhouse

Leeds Playhouse has been one of the UK's leading producing theatres for 55 years. It is an award-winning theatre and a cultural hub, a place where people gather to tell and share stories and engage in world-class theatre. It makes work which is pioneering and relevant, seeking out the best companies and artists to create inspirational theatre in the heart of Yorkshire.

2025 was a fantastic year for Leeds Playhouse, with its productions and performers receiving national recognition in the UK's most prestigious theatre awards. Its co-production of *Animal Farm* won Best Play Revival at the UK Theatre Awards and was nominated as Best New Production in Affiliate Theatre at the Olivier Awards; at the WhatsOnStage Awards, *Through It All Together* was nominated for Best Regional Production and Best New Play; its co-production of *Sisters 360* was nominated for Best Stage Production at the Asian Media Awards; Cash Holland won Best Supporting Female Actor in a Play for *A Raisin in the Sun* at the Black British Theatre Awards; and Shobna Gulati was nominated for *Through It All Together* at the Asian Media Awards.

In previous years, the Playhouse's warm welcome was recognised at the UK Theatre Awards in 2022, when it was named Most Welcoming Theatre, highlighting its daily endeavours to make the building an inviting, engaging, creative, accessible and inclusive hub at the heart of the Leeds City Region. For three consecutive years, leading performers in Playhouse productions were named Best Performer in a Musical at the UK Theatre Awards and, in 2024, its production of *Oliver!* was named Best Musical.

Alongside the work on its stages, the Playhouse works creatively with the people, artists and communities of Leeds through its innovative, sector-leading Playhouse Connect programme. Focusing on two key areas – Learning & Skills and Creative Communities – Playhouse Connect engages with thousands of people in the region each year. As part of this work, its Artistic Development programme, Furnace, engages with theatre-makers, providing a creative space to refine their practice at all stages of their careers; it builds, develops and sustains projects to connect with refugee communities, young people and students, older people and people with learning disabilities; it hands over spaces to communities to use in ways they choose, from breakdancing to roller-skating, craft markets to tea parties, enlivening the building whilst fostering deeper relationships; and works in-residence around the city, connecting with people on their doorsteps.

As a registered charity, Leeds Playhouse relies on the support of valued partners to make great things happen. It is grateful for the continued support of Arts Council England, Leeds City Council, The Liz and Terry Bramall Foundation and the many charitable trusts, business partners and individuals that continue to support the vital work of the theatre.

About Unicorn Theatre

Transforming young lives through theatre.

At the Unicorn, we create new, inventive and enthralling theatre experiences for children aged up to 13. Every year, we welcome over 60,000 families and schools through our doors, and many thousands more through Unicorn Online.

We believe that young people of all ages, perspectives and abilities have the right to experience exciting, entertaining and inspiring work and we actively seek out children who wouldn't otherwise attend, offering free tickets where needed. Through our Creative Hub, we develop productions with children from our local partner schools and communities to ensure that our work remains relevant and informed by the young people we serve. To read more, visit unicorntheatre.com

The Unicorn Theatre is a registered charity and relies on the generous support of donors. Planet Omar, *as part of our Weston Theatre season, was made possible with special thanks to Charles Holloway OBE, Weston Theatre Season Partner.*

About Birmingham Repertory Theatre

Birmingham Rep has been at the forefront of theatre in the UK for over 100 years. The Rep has an unparalleled pioneering history and is the only producing theatre in the UK's Second City. It is the oldest building-based theatre company in the UK, and the forerunner of both the RSC and the National Theatre.

The Rep's mission is to create artistically ambitious, world-class theatre for everyone. The commissioning and production of new work that is proudly made in Birmingham here at The Rep lies at the core of the theatre's programme, and over the last 15 years the company has produced more than 130 new plays.

The Rep's acclaimed Creative Learning and Talent Development programme is one of the largest and most diverse of any arts organisation in the country. The Rep has nurtured new talent throughout its history – from Laurence Olivier and Peter Brook to its modern-day youth theatre, and the ground-breaking Rep Foundry theatre-makers programme, it has offered opportunity and training for thousands of early career writers, directors and artists.

2025 Rep highlights include a sold-out production and following community tour of *Community* written by proud Brummie and Rep Foundry alumnus, Farrah Chaudhry, and a sold-out new production of Khaled Hosseini's *A Thousand Splendid Suns* co-produced with Leeds Playhouse and Nottingham Playhouse.

Artistic Director of The Rep Joe Murphy's inaugural 2026 Spring season includes the world premiere of *Sherlock Holmes and the 12 Days of Christmas* written by Humphrey Ker and David Reed with original songs by Tim Rice and Andrew Lloyd Webber; Jodie Comer's reprisal of her Olivier-winning performance in a sold-out one-week- only production of *Prima Facie*; following the success of *A Thousand Splendid Suns*, The Rep presents a stage adaptation of Andrea Levy's *Small Island* with Leeds Playhouse and Nottingham Playhouse, in association with Actors Touring Company; and two Rep-made productions directed by Joe himself – *A Midsummer Night's Dream* and *Sweeney Todd: The Demon Barber of Fleet Street*.

Many of The Rep's productions and co-productions go on to have lives beyond Birmingham. The theatre's long-running production of *The Snowman* celebrated its 30th anniversary in 2024, alongside its forthcoming 27th consecutive season at London's Peacock Theatre. Since 2021, other Rep tours and transfers have included *Inspector Morse: House of Ghosts*, *A Thousand Splendid Suns*, *Community*, *Of Mice and Men*, *Idiots Assemble: Spitting Image the Musical*, *The Way Old Friends Do*, *The Play What I Wrote*, *Animal Farm* and *East Is East*.

About Hachette Children's Group

Hachette Children's Group is one of the largest children's publishers in the UK, with an outstanding track record in creating bestselling and award-winning books for children and young people. The Group is committed to raising readers whatever their age, stage or interest, with vibrant lists offering a book for every child, including baby and pre-school books, picture books, gift, fiction, non-fiction, books for the school and library market and licensed publishing.

HCG comprises the imprints Orchard Books, Starboard, Tempest, Blyton Books, Wren & Rook, Welbeck Children's Books, Laurence King Publishing, Franklin Watts and Wayland.

The Group publishes a wide range of authors, illustrators, series and licences including: A.B. Hamilton, Adiba Jaigirdar, Alex T. Smith, Alex Wheatle, Alexandra Bracken, Alice Oseman, Cariad Lloyd, Chris Chatterton, Chris Smith, Cressida Cowell, David Almond, Dean Atta, Dermot O'Leary, Forest Xiao, Francesca Simon, Gabby's Dollhouse, Giles Andreae, Guy Parker-Rees, Jacqueline Wilson, Jennifer Lynn Barnes, Jessica Townsend, Jim Field, J.J. Arcanjo, J.K. Rowling, Julian Gough, Kes Gray, Kiran Millwood Hargrave, L. D. Lapinski, Laini Taylor, Lauren Child, Lauren St John, Leigh Bardugo, Matt Goodfellow, Matt Oldfield, Matthew Syed, Mike Brownlow, Neil Coslett, Official Mr Bean, Onjali Q. Raúf, Piers Torday, Rachel Bright, Rainbow Magic, Ramzee, Rev. Richard Coles, Robert Muchamore, Simon Mugford, Simon Rickerty, Siobhan McDermott, The Magic Pet Shop, Tom Tinn Disbury, Yassmin Abdel-Magied and Zanib Mian.

Hachette Children's Group is also the owner of Enid Blyton Entertainment.

Previous HCG imprints include Hodder Children's Books, Orion Children's Books, Quercus Children's Books and Little, Brown Books for Young Readers.

Zanib Mian's

Planet Omar

Adapted for the stage by Asif Khan

For my friend Abdul Shayek
Former Artistic Director of Tara Theatre
3 March 1984 to 1 August 2023

Characters

Omar *(actor one)*

Mum, **Laura** *(actor two)*

Dad, **Homeless Man**, **Reza**, **James** *(actor three)*

Maryam, **Daniel** *(actor four)*

Mrs Rodgers, **Mrs Hutchinson**, **Mosque Woman** *(actor five)*

Charlie, **Daniel's Mum**, **Esa** *(actor six)*

The character of Esa is a puppet, played by actor six. An ensemble will be required throughout.

Setting

London

Notes

A forward slash (/) = an interruption.

Beat = short pause.

Pause = slightly longer.

Silence = even longer.

Act One

Scene One

In darkness.

Omar *runs on in a panic, being chased by a figure.*

Omar I was being chased!

Through the school corridors . . . by a teacher!

Not an ordinary teacher, no.

We see a teacher with green slime oozing out of its ears and slugs for fingernails. Or something equally scary. It calls out **Omar***'s name.* **Omar** *runs.*

I flung through doors . . . past school bags . . . smashed through lunch boxes . . . whizzed by lockers . . . and finally burst into the playground.

But the monster teacher thing was still right behind me!

Omar *trips.*

Woooaaah!

Omar *lands on the ground.*

Don't eat me! Please don't eat me!

The teacher figure gets closer.

Aaahhh!

School bell rings.

But then I woke up. It was a dream!

Slimy teacher disappears.

Kind of extremely and very happy that I wasn't about to be a monster's dinner.

I remembered that my mum told me if I have a nightmare . . . 'spit towards your left shoulder three times . . . and the shaytan will disappear'. Shaytan is the devil . . . the ugly head who makes bad dreams.

Voiceover of a scary shaytan laughing.

Omar So I did. I spat.

Omar *conjures up a bucketful of spit in his mouth and then launches it like an Olympic athlete.*

Omar But it missed shaytan and . . .

We see **Esa**, *crying.*

Esa WAAAAAA AAAAAAAAAAHH!

Omar My little brother. It landed on my little brother!

A ping sound freezes the action, apart from **Omar**.

Omar Don't be fooled by this two-year-old's face . . . he always takes my stuff . . . and makes it all sticky.

A ping sound unfreezes the action.

Esa WAAAAAA AAAAAAAAAAHH!

Omar Hush, Esa! Please!

Mum *rushes in wearing her pyjamas.*

Mum What's going on?!

A ping sound freezes the action, apart from **Omar**.

Omar You can recognise an unimpressed parent because they always have one hand on their hip . . . like this (*He points it out on a frozen* **Mum**.) And the eyebrows are pointing down . . . like this. It can be very scary.

This is Mum. She's a scientist . . . who is normally never seen without a cup of coffee in her hand. She looks like this at home . . . but she puts a hijab on when she goes out.

A ping sound unfreezes the action.

Esa WAAAAAA AAAAAAAAAAHH!

Mum What have you done, Omar?!

She goes to **Esa** *to comfort him.*

Omar Spitball.

Mum Not again, Omar! I told you that you don't actually spit . . . it's just . . .

She demonstrates how it's actually supposed to be done, while dealing with **Esa**, *who continues crying.*

Dad *enters in his pyjamas.*

Dad What's going on?

Omar/Mum Spitball.

Dad Again?!

A ping freezes action.

Omar Dad . . . who has a beard . . . because he's copying the greatest man who ever lived . . . Prophet Muhammad . . . peace be upon him . . . I've never actually seen his face without it. A scientist as well. Who hates beetroot . . . and says he doesn't have much hair left . . . cos of his genes . . . so sometimes he wears a mosque hat . . . and sometimes he wears a helmet . . . cos he rides a motorbike.

A ping unfreezes.

Esa WAAAAAA AAAAAAAAAAHH!

Dad It would be nice, Omar . . . if we could have at least one night in the week where poor Esa isn't woken up by your shenanigans.

Omar What does 'shenanigans' mean?

Dad *rolls his eyes, takes* **Esa** *from* **Mum**, *and exits, while comforting him.*

Omar What does 'shenanigans' mean, Dad?!

Maryam *enters in a sleepy grump.*

Maryam What's all the noise for . . . I'm sleeping!

A ping freezes.

Omar My sister. Maryam. Who is thirteen . . . but thinks she's sixteen. Alright . . . she knows twenty-eight sections of the Qur'an by heart . . . which is fairly impressive . . . but she's still annoying when she tries to wind me up. And once, she got caught hiding a stash of fondant fancies under her pillow. Naughty naughty!

A ping unfreezes.

Mum Nothing, Maryam . . . go back to bed.

Maryam *exits.*

Mum (*to* **Dad**) Is it almost time for Fajr?

Dad (*off-stage*) In ten minutes.

Mum Right.

Omar So it's good that I woke you up?

Mum Why?

Omar It's morning prayer time anyway!

Mum No, it's not good, Omar.

Omar Will Allah give me a reward for waking you up for Fajr prayer?

Mum Come on. Back to sleep.

She exits, leaving **Omar** *alone.*

Omar Well, I think I deserve a reward. Right . . . back to sleep.

My name is Omar. In case you didn't catch on. I love pain au chocolat and I hate marshmallows.

Right . . . back to sleep.

Oh and once I raced against my dad's car on my bike . . . and won! Right, sleep.

With hopefully, no more 'shenanigans'!

Scene Two

Alarm sound.

Omar (*sings*) Gooood mooorning . . . gooood mooorning . . . gooood mooorning!

Mum Full of energy as usual.

Omar I'm on full charge!

Mum Does your battery ever die?

Omar Never!

Mum No more bad dreams?

Omar Just seventy-seven. Maybe seventy-eight. Sometimes it was about a slimy teacher with slugs for fingernails. And sometimes it was an evil robotic teacher with red eyes. Or an octopus teacher with eight arms.

Mum Poor thing. You're feeling nervous about starting your new school aren't you?

Omar I've got snakes in my tummy.

Mum Butterflies?

Omar It feels like snakes. And some of them sneak up and squeeze my heart.

Mum Poor baby. It's a big change for you all.

Mum *kisses* **Omar** *and exits.*

Omar (*to audience*) It would be so much more convenient and better for everybody if things always just stayed the same. Take my pyjamas, for example. They are utterly comfortable pyjamas. But Mum tried to throw them away and make me wear crispy new ones!

This is change. It's super-annoying. One big, fat, huge change was already happening to me . . .

We're moving house!

We used to live in a place called Whitechapel . . . (*We hear the soundscape of Whitechapel.*) Which had lots of people and shops and noisy cars all over the place.

But now we were moving to a whole new different house . . . in a place called Harrow. (*We hear the soundscape of Harrow.*) Which just has lots of big houses . . . and you don't hear anything but birds tweeting everywhere!

This is the reason I have to start a new school. It's all Mum's fault cos she got her 'dream job'. When she told me I was confused. Did it mean that adults have super-boring dreams all about jobs? If that was true I wouldn't be looking forward to being an adult . . . no way . . . cos now . . . I dream about fun stuff like being on a roller coaster!

He pretends he's on a roller coaster.

Woooooaaaaahhhhh! Hold on, we're coming to the big dip!

He goes down the imaginary big dip.

Aaaaaahhhhh! This rollercoaster is ace . . . but now it's gonna turn into a . . . a flying pig.

He's now on a flying pig.

We're high up in the sky (*Pointing.*) I can see Big Ben there! And Buckingham Palace there! Oh . . . and look . . . it's Croydon!

Back to normality.

Omar So anyway . . . we had to move. And moving was very, very, times one hundred, annoying. Because Dad said /

Dad *enters.*

Dad You can't take all the 1,267 bits and bobs and toys from your room to the new house.

Omar Did you actually count the toys?

Dad No.

Omar You just like to say exact numbers when you're talking so you can sound smart.

Dad Cheeky! Just choose the ones you love most and we'll give the rest to charity.

Omar But I love them all!

Dad I'll be very proud of you if you could choose.

Omar (*to audience*) I like it when dad's proud of me cos it normally means . . . pain au chocolat!

Fifteen minutes later.

Omar Dad! I did it!

Dad What?

Omar I've chosen fifty-six bits and bobs to take with me.

Dad Exactly fifty-six?

Omar Yeah! I counted them!

Dad That's my boy.

Omar Pain au chocolat?

Dad Fine.

Omar Yes! (*To audience.*) I wonder if he'd give me two pain au chocolats if I got it down to forty-six? The good thing about moving to a new house was . . .

Lighting and sound change. They're now in the new house.

Mum, **Esa** *and* **Maryam** *join* **Omar** *and* **Dad**.

Omar It's massive!

Maryam The garden is massive!

Omar This new house is super-cool!

Maryam Look, I can do my goal celebration without smacking my arm on the fence!

Dad We can put a football goal for you there, Maryam.

Maryam Yes!

Dad And your own little veg patch there, Omar.

Omar Yes!

Mum And a climbing frame here for Esa!

Esa Climey . . . climey!

Dad Come on, Esa . . . you haven't seen your bedroom yet.

Mum You're going to love your room, Esa!

Esa Roomy . . . roomy!

Dad *takes* **Esa** *inside.*

Mum So d'you like it?

Maryam I mean . . . it's alright.

Mum Just alright?

Omar Alright times one hundred.

Mum Not a thousand?

Omar Just a hundred.

Mum *spots the next-door neighbor,* **Mrs Rodgers**.

Mum (*cheerfully*) Oh hello . . . we're the new neighbours!

Mrs Rodgers *just stares.*

Mum Lovely to meet you!

Mrs Rodgers *continues to just stare. Then walks off.*

Maryam She's nice.

Omar Why did she put her nose in the air like that?

Maryam Maybe she was smelling something she didn't like.

Scene Three

Sound of an alarm clock.

Omar (*to audience*) Saturday!

Two more sleeps till I start school on Monday. Two more sleeps before I walk into a brand-new classroom. With everyone watching. And a teacher who might or might not be . . . (*a scary sound*) an Alien Zombie. Or possibly . . . (*a scary sound*) a Space Crocodile. Or maybe . . . (*a scary sound*) a Robotic Lizard.

Sound of a tube train approaching the platform.

Voiceover This is the Bakerloo Line. Please mind the gap.

Omar (*laughing*) 'Please mind the gap!'

Mum Come on, kids. Hop on.

Sound of the busy carriage.

Maryam Where are we going?

Mum Baker Street. There's a lovely mosque there.

Maryam But I'm tired.

Omar Is that where they bake bread?

Esa Bready . . . bready!

Mum That's a good question . . . why do they call it 'Baker Street'?

Omar I can google it!

Mum Anyway, I want to take you to a different mosque every Saturday.

Omar After we pray Dhuhr can we go to a cafe and get a pain au chocolat?

Esa Chocolatey . . . Chocolatey!

Mum Yes. And Maryam . . . I'll buy you a fondant fancy.

Maryam Ok then.

Mum We can explore a whole new part of town. Not too far from here . . . is where Mummy's new job is!

Omar (*to audience*) Mum is very smart and works out all sorts of different ways of fighting cancer for the cancer research people.

Esa Smoothie . . . smoothie!

Mum You've just had one, Esa.

Esa Thirsty thirsty!

Mum Ok then.

Omar (*to audience*) But sometimes Esa's cuteness makes her lose her smartness. It's like he has big smartness melting eyes. So when Esa wanted to buy a whistle from this shop /

Esa Whistle . . . whistle!

Omar I knew it wasn't a good idea /

Esa Pleasie . . . pleasie!

Omar But Mum went right ahead and bought it for him saying . . .

Mum Because you've been such a good boy this morning!

Mum *gives* **Esa** *a gooey kiss on his head.*

Esa Kissy . . . kissy!

Omar I know that kiss is gooey, cos she actually kisses me like that.

Mum And one kiss for Maryam . . . and one kiss for Omar.

Omar Please don't ever do that in front of my friends, Mum.

Voiceover This is Baker Street.

Maryam Mum . . . we've gotta get off.

Voiceover Please mind the gap.

They jump off the tube train.

We hear the sound of the Adhaan, call to prayer.

Omar (*to audience*) At the mosque, everyone prays together with the imaam leading. It's supposed to be super-quiet.

They all stand in line and start the prayer together.

Imaam Allahu Akbar.

All (*hands just above shoulders*) Allahu Akbar.

We hear the imaam repeat 'Allahu Akbar' just before the Rukhu and Sujood.

Esa *is sat next to* **Mum**, *watching, as they begin to pray.*

He begins to look around.

Omar *is distracted by him, but continues with his prayer.* **Esa** *begins walking round them, through their legs, etc.*

They go into the next prayer position, Rukhu. Hands on knees. **Esa** *tries to copy this action.*

They go into the next prayer position, Sujood. Nose and forehead on the ground. **Esa** *tries to copy this action too.*

Then decides to climb on **Mum***'s back.*

They are all trying to pray but **Esa** *is proving to be a real distraction. They all stand after the Sujood.*

Esa *wanders off. Then . . . he pulls out his whistle and blows loudly!*

Esa One, two, three, four, five!

Blows.

Mum Esa!

Esa One, two, three, four, five!

Esa *blows again.*

Then keeps repeating.

Blow, count, blow, count. **Omar** *laughs hysterically.*

Maryam Stop laughing, Omar!

Mum *has no choice but to stop praying and see to* **Esa**.

Mum Esa! Stop it!

She grabs **Esa** *and they all start to exit the prayer hall. Embarrassed.*

Heads down.

Omar Why is your face gone a bright shade of pink, Mum?

Maryam Shut up, Omar.

Omar And yours, Maryam?

Maryam I said shut up.

Omar It's like your skin has decided to compete with your socks for pinkness, Maryam.

Mum Both of you hush! Let's go!

She continues to guide them out.

Scene Four

Dad *enters.*

Dad *(in a big booming voice)* It's Science Sunday!

Omar *(to audience)* Dad always does that. *(To* **Dad**.*)* Why do you always do that, Dad?

Dad Because . . . it's *(in a big booming voice)* Science Sunday!

Omar I think he and Mum only had us three kids so they could create more scientists or something. But I actually do like 'Science Sundays'. *(To* **Dad**.*)* Can we make slime again, Dad?

Dad Not this Sunday.

Omar What about the fizzy eruption?

Maryam We did that last time, Omar.

Mum *enters with a tray of various science materials and places them on the table.*

Omar *(to audience)* Mum always wants everything done very precisely and says things like . . .

Mum Just one millilitre more, my cotton button.

Omar Or . . .

Mum Are you sure you stirred that correctly, sunshine?

Dad *laughs.*

Dad *kisses* **Mum***'s head.*

Dad That's why she's the best scientist in the world.

Mum *kisses* **Dad***'s hand and smiles.*

Omar Super-yuck.

Maryam *suddenly drops something.*

Maryam Oops! Sorry!

Omar Maryam always does that.

Dad It's ok, darling.

Esa, *who has been crawling in the background, approaches and steps on what* **Maryam** *has just dropped.*

Dad Esa! Careful! You play over here with this, Esa.

He hands **Esa** *a toy to play with.*

Mum Ok . . . so this Sunday we're going to do 'Tornados in Bottles'.

Omar So cool!

Mum (*demonstrating*) You connect the two bottles with a little pipe like this . . . and then you whirl the top bottle . . . which makes the water go down to the bottom bottle . . . and sends air up . . . making a . . .

Maryam Tornado!

Omar I wanna go! I wanna go! Pass the bipes!

Maryam (*laughs*) Bipes?

They all laugh.

Omar I mean pipes. Bottle and pipes.

Maryam Bipes!

Omar I just said it wrong.

Maryam But I like it!

Omar I do actually. It should be a real word!

Maryam If it was a real word, then it would just be normal and you wouldn't like it any more.

Dad That's true. In Arabic, there's no 'p' sound, so a pipe would end up being called /

Mum/Dad A bibe!

They laugh and keep repeating 'bibe!'.

Omar (*to audience*) You can see . . . there's enough fun and chaos on 'Science Sundays' to keep your mind distracted. Enough to stop me thinking about Monday. But the day zoomed by and . . .

Scene Five

Morning alarm sounds.

Omar Monday!

He lies down.

My lungs are pushing air out of me . . . but not taking any back in. And my stomach is like a giant heavy rock . . . so I can't get out of bed. What if nobody likes me? What if the work is harder than at my last school? What if nobody wants to be my friend? What if the teacher is an alien?!

Maryam *enters.*

Maryam Wake up, lazy head, and stop pretending to be sick.

Omar I'm not!

Dad *enters.*

Maryam He's pretending to be sick.

Omar My lungs are feeling strange.

Dad Come on.

He picks **Omar** *up and plonks him down in front of a bowl of porridge.*

Omar (*to audience*) Porridge. Now I know what you might be thinking . . . yuck! But actually . . . when you put biscuit spread on it . . . it tastes alright. (*To* **Dad**.) There's a rock in my tummy.

Ensemble take off the porridge bowl.

Dad You're gonna be totally fine. The teacher will make sure you make friends. Now hurry along, your mum's getting stressed about you being late.

Ensemble help him get dressed.

Omar (*to audience*) There was no uniform at this school, so I was allowed to wear what I wanted. My favourite sweatshirt. My favourite jeans. This stain here . . . is from when Esa threw a barbecue chicken wing at me. Oh well.

Finishes getting dressed.

Right, I'm ready, Mum!

Omar *walks up to* **Mum**, *who stares at him.*

Mum I don't believe it. I don't believe it. I don't believe it. I don't believe it. I don't believe it.

Omar (*counting along on his hand*) She said it five times.

Dad Son, I think Mum has given you clean, ironed clothes to wear . . . so go and put them on please. Quickly, or you'll be late.

Omar Ok.

Ensemble rush back on and change him again.

Omar (*to audience*) Now it felt like my tummy had a million frogs hopping about in it . . . just waiting to leap up my throat. So I imagined . . . a super-awesome, magnificent, dragon!

Music.

A giant dragon enters played by the cast – a puppet. **Omar** *hops on it.*

Omar A much better way to get to school! Forget driving in Mum's car. He could fly me there at 120 mph!

The dragon takes **Omar** *to school at speed.*

Omar You have arrived at your destination!

The dragon breathes out a plume of steam and lets down **Omar**.

Omar I pronounce thee 'H20'! That's a good name for him I think. My parents will be happy with that name . . . that's the kind of science-y thing they love to talk about!

H20! What are you doing, you silly?!

H20 appears being silly. **Omar** *laughs. H20 disappears.*

Mrs Hutchinson Welcome, Omar! Welcome to your new school and your new class! Say hello, everyone . . . this is Omar.

Voiceover Hello, Omar.

Omar Mrs Hutchinson has amazing hair. It changes depending on her mood.

The ensemble place a magnificent wig on **Mrs Hutchinson**, *which resembles the way* **Omar** *sees it. From now on we always see* **Mrs Hutchinson** *in her magnificent wig.*

Omar When she's happy, those curls bounce. When she's tired, they flop down. When she's cross, they look more like the twisty metal part of a drill. Woah. Imagine a drill-headed Mrs Hutchinson making a hole in the wall!

He stares obsessively at her hair.

Mrs Hutchinson Oh. Do I have something in my hair?

Omar You have cool hair.

Mrs Hutchinson Why thank you. Why don't you sit down here . . . next to Charlie.

Omar Hi, Charlie.

Charlie Hi.

Omar My name is Omar.

Charlie Ok.

Omar What's this school like?

Charlie It's ok.

Omar Oh. What's this class like?

Charlie It's ok.

Omar Is the playground good?

Charlie You mean when it's dry or when it's wet?

Omar Erm. Dry?

Charlie It's ok.

Omar Wet?

Charlie Ok.

Omar I decided that 'ok' was Charlie's favourite word.

Is there anything that is not 'ok'?

Charlie Yes.

Omar What?

Charlie Daniel.

Omar Daniel?

Charlie Daniel. That boy over there. He's the one you have to look out for, ok?

Omar Ok.

Charlie Just stay out of his way.

Omar Ok. There's just a little problem?

Charlie What?

Omar Every time my mum tells me to stay away from something I always seem to be drawn towards it.

Charlie Like a magnet?

Omar Like a trouble magnet.

Charlie Like what?

Omar Like when I was told not to open my sister's secret box . . . and then I just had to.

Charlie So what happened?

Omar A gazillion million teeny tiny beads came pouring out, all over her bedroom floor, just as she walked in.

Charlie What did she do?

Omar Screamed.

Charlie Oh.

Omar So I hope I don't do the same kind of magnet thing with Daniel.

Charlie Oh no.

Omar What?

Charlie Daniel's coming.

Omar Where?

Charlie Here!

A quick blast of music – something representing the presence of danger. And we see **Daniel**.

He wanders over to **Omar** *and* **Charlie**, *while they hold their breath.*

Daniel The new kid and the weird kid sitting together. How nice.

Omar Thanks.

Daniel Why did you say 'thanks'?

Omar Because you said it was 'nice'.

Charlie He didn't mean it that way.

Omar Oh. Were you speaking upside down?

Daniel What?

Omar Actually you must have been cos you called Charlie the 'weird kid'.

Daniel You're both weird kids. Idiots!

He exits.

Charlie See? He's always horrible to me.

Omar Why? Did you two have a fight about something?

Charlie No. He just hates me for no reason.

Omar Just you?

Charlie Well, he hates you now as well. I think he hates the whole class actually. But he hates me the most. Then you second.

Omar Don't be sad. I don't hate you.

Charlie Ok.

School bell rings.

Omar (*to audience*) Home time!

Mum *and* **Omar** *walking home.*

Mum I'm so pleased you had a good first day! I had a good first day too. On my dream job.

Omar What did you do?

Mum Mostly poking at microscopic stuff with fancy equipment. Then on the way back I bought this.

It's a box of chocolates.

Omar For me?!

Mum Not for you, pumpkin. But I've got another bar for you in my bag. I got this box for our new neighbour.

Omar The new neighbour who stuck her nose in the air?

Mum Yes.

Omar Like she smelt something she didn't like?

Mum Well, we might have misread the situation. So I bought this. We can pop round when we get home . . . say hello properly.

Omar Ok, Mum. (*To audience.*) We picked up Maryam.

Maryam *joins them.*

Omar (*to audience*) And we picked up the little human thing we call a brother from nursery.

Esa *joins them.*

Mum (*to* **Esa**) What are you like? Always half your lunch on your jumper.

Omar (*to audience*) Mum is embarrassed to have mucky kids.

Mum Wait. Let me hair your run through my fingers.

Omar Sometimes Mum says things the wrong way round when she's hurrying.

Maryam You mean 'run your fingers' through his hair?

Omar And Maryam always likes to correct her.

Mum Yes, yes, that.

Omar (*to audience*) We got to Mrs Rodgers' door.

Mum Ok.

She takes a deep breath and rings the doorbell. No response.

She rings again.

No response.

Omar Do it like this!

He bangs on the door really loud.

Mum Why did you do that?!

Omar Maybe the doorbell isn't working.

Mum It's rude!

Mrs Rodgers *opens the door opens slowly.*

Mum/Maryam/Omar Hello!

Esa Assalamu-alaikum!

Omar Our naani taught him how to say that.

Mrs Rodgers *doesn't respond. She just stands there and stares. After a few seconds . . .*

Mum We're the new neighbours. Just thought we'd come over and introduce ourselves.

Still no response from **Mrs Rodgers**.

Maryam (*whispers to* **Omar**) OMG, this is so awkward!

Omar (*whispers to* **Maryam**) OMG, I know!

Mum My name's Aisha. May I ask your name?

Mrs Rodgers Rodgers.

She then slams the door. A few seconds.

Mum *is stunned.*

Omar Mum?

Mum Yes?

Omar Can I have the box of chocolates then?

Scene Six

An alarm clock.

Dad Did you brush your teeth?

Omar Yes.

Dad Back ones too?

Omar Yes.

Dad Sure?

Omar Yes, Dad.

Dad Have you done your duas?

Omar Yes.

Dad Good.

Omar Dad?

Dad Yes?

Omar Do you think people wonder what Muslims might be doing when they see their lips moving?

Dad What?

Omar When we're doing our duas and talking to Allah. Do you think they might be wondering if we're talking to ourselves?

Dad You don't even need to move your lips. Just say it in your head and Allah will always hear you.

Omar (*to audience*) There are duas for everything . . . eating, sleeping, waking up, knowledge, leaving the house, coming back into the house . . . basically anything you can think of. I used to forget, but now I made sure I did them . . . especially the 'prayer for protection'. Because Daniel was getting meaner everyday. I needed all the help I could get.

School bell rings.

Omar *is now at school with* **Charlie**, *in the playground.*

Daniel *is following them around, not saying anything, but occasionally making the odd grunting sound.*

Omar *and* **Charlie** *are clearly uncomfortable. Then suddenly* **Daniel** *charges at them both.* **Charlie** *jumps.*

Daniel *starts laughing like a mad man. The school bell sounds.*

Daniel *exits.*

They're in the classroom.

Omar Well, that was an ok playtime wasn't it?

Charlie Better than yesterday at least.

Mrs Hutchinson Right, everyone! So we were looking at some paintings by a particular famous painter last time . . . can you remember his name?

Charlie Picasso!

Mrs Hutchinson That's correct. So this time you're going to paint a self-portrait. Do you know what a 'self-portrait' is?

Charlie It's when you draw a picture of yourself.

Mrs Hutchinson That's right. However, I want you to have a go at making your own self-portraits in the same style as Picasso!

They start drawing.

Omar Ha!

Charlie What?

Omar These are funny!

Charlie Mine's got a triangle green nose!

Omar Mine's got weird-shaped eyes!

Daniel *walks past and sends the dirty water pot tumbling onto* **Omar***'s painting.*

Daniel Oops. Clumsy me.

Omar Was that an accident or are you talking upside-down again?

Daniel What?

Omar Was it an 'oops' moment?

Charlie No.

Omar Or was it a 'let's ruin Omar's painting moment'?

Charlie Yes.

Daniel Weirdos!

He exits.

Charlie He's just a big frogspawn head.

Omar He spoilt my painting.

Charlie I bet you can paint a new one even better!

Omar Hey, I just thought something.

Charlie What?

Omar What if some kid had ruined Picasso's painting at school one day, which is why it came out all different and weird and that's what made him famous?

Charlie Then I think you could be famous!

Omar *and* **Charlie** *continue painting.*

Mrs Hutchinson Omar! You did this?!

Omar Yes, Miss.

Mrs Hutchinson It's . . . wow. It's brilliant! I love how you've used water to add that blurring effect . . . I'm so impressed.

She exits.

Charlie Daniel's looking at us again.

Omar I know. His face looks funny.

Charlie It doesn't look like a happy face.

Omar It looks like that face you make when you accidentally touch someone's old chewing gum.

Daniel *approaches.*

Charlie He's coming!

Daniel *hands* **Omar** *a piece of paper with a note. Then leaves.*

Charlie What does it say?

Omar 'Watch out'.

Charlie Oh dear.

School bell sounds.

Omar *is home.*

Omar (*to audience*) Home. (*To* **Mum**.) I know that smell, Mum!

Mum I'm making your favourite food!

Omar You mean my all-time favourite Pakistani food?

Mum That's right.

Omar Biryani?!

Mum Yes.

Omar How did you magically know that I really wanted biryani tonight?!

Mum I'm your mum. I know everything.

Omar Biryani always cheers me up.

Mum That's why I'm making it!

Omar Can you make it every week, Mum?

Mum I'm afraid scientists with full-time jobs don't have the time to make it that often. It's hard to make. Can you open the door?

Omar It's cold.

Mum I can't have the house smelling of food.

Omar Use air freshener.

Mum Homes are meant to smell of nothing. Not food . . . or weird artificial air fresheners.

Omar *opens the doors, whilst* **Mum** *continues with the cooking.*

Omar I can see Mrs Rodgers.

Mum Don't stare.

Omar She's poking around at her weeds with one wrinkly hand and holding the phone with the other.

Mum Stop staring at her.

Mrs Rodgers John, the Muslims are frying smelly onions again!

Omar Mum, I think she doesn't like /

Mum I heard!

Omar Dad doesn't like the smell either.

Mum Let's send her some.

Omar She said she doesn't like the smell /

Mum I know it gets really stinky when it's cooking, but it's yummy when you eat it.

Omar Mum, I don't think she deserves some of our delicious dinner.

Mum Well, she's going to get some. And you can take it round to her.

Omar What?

Fast forward and **Omar** *is now at* **Mrs Rodgers'** *front door with a container full of biryani. He knocks.*

No answer.

Omar She always takes ages to answer the door.

He knocks again.

Mrs Rodgers *answers.*

Omar Hi. My mum made this for you.

Mrs Rodgers Spicy food? No thank you!

She shuts her door.

Omar Sheeeeeeesh. You'd think we were trying to poison her.

Scene Seven

Dad Charlie's here!

Omar Hi, Charlie!

Charlie Hi, Omar.

Dad It's nice to finally meet you, Charlie. I've been hearing so much about you!

Charlie Oh thank you, Omar's daddy.

Dad It's lovely to have you over . . . and you can come any time you want.

Omar Dad was being so cheesy. I wonder what he might look like if he was made of cheese.

The ensemble make **Dad** *look like a block of cheese.* **Dad** *looks like cheese for the rest of this scene.*

Dad Now Omar told me you're happy with pizza?

Charlie I love pizza, thank you.

Omar Every kid loves pizza.

Dad I think the whole world might love pizza . . . don't you?

Charlie Well . . . I've never met a person who doesn't like pizza.

Dad Me neither! Right I'll get them in the oven then!

He exits.

Omar I was really excited about you coming.

Charlie I was as well. We can play and talk and have fun, with no Daniel around.

Omar Yeah, I think this is the least terrified I've ever seen you look. Ever.

Charlie I think he's starting to make our days 60 per cent bad.

Omar Maybe 70 per cent.

Charlie Before it was 40 per cent . . . but he's been extra grumpy and mean lately.

Omar I wonder what's making him so grumpy and mean?

Charlie Maybe he keeps slipping on rotten apples.

Omar What?

Charlie You know the really sludgy and soft ones. They make you slip more than banana skins.

Omar More than banana skins?

Charlie Maybe the more rotten apples he slips on . . . the worse he feels . . . and the more mean he gets.

Omar Maybe.

Charlie Or maybe they're rotten plums.

Omar Well . . . there has to be something.

Charlie Your dad's not putting plums on the pizza is he?

Omar I don't think they put plums on pizza.

Charlie Not keen on plums.

Omar I hate plums as well.

Charlie Or peanuts, or coconuts, or bananas, or cinnamon, or coffee!

Omar Luckily I don't think they put any of those on pizza. You're not allergic to cheese are you?

Charlie No I love cheese.

Omar My cousin Reza is and he does lots of farts and gets a really bad tummy ache if he eats cheese.

Maryam *approaches.*

Maryam Is this your friend, Omar?

Omar Yes. His name is Charlie.

Charlie What's your name?

Maryam Maryam. Do you want to play football?

Charlie Yeah!

Maryam Come to the garden then.

They're in the garden.

We see **Mrs Rodgers**, *who dials on her phone.*

Omar Maryam, pass!

Maryam You have to take it off me!

Charlie Tackle her, Omar!

Omar I'm trying!

Maryam I'm too good!

Omar Tackle her, Charlie!

Charlie I'm trying! She's too good!

Maryam I can beat both of you!

Mrs Rodgers I can hear the Muslims, John . . . they're being noisy again.

Omar Let's both try and tackle together!

Maryam That's the goal there!

Mrs Rodgers I mean really, why can't they play quietly like good children?

Omar Don't let her score!

Charlie Shall I be goalie?

Omar Yeah!

Maryam *kicks towards the goal and scores.*

Omar/Charlie (*loudly*) Nooooo!

Maryam (*singing loudly*) It's coming home . . . it's coming home . . . it's coming . . . football's coming home!

Mrs Rodgers Honestly . . . I can't take this much ridiculous noise.

Maryam, **Omar** *and* **Charlie** *look at each other. Then burst out laughing and run inside.*

Scene Eight

School bell.

It's lunchtime.

Omar *and* **Charlie** *sat with their lunch boxes.*

Charlie Rotten plums or rotten apricots?

Omar What?

Charlie Or rotten gooseberries? What's worse to slip on . . . rotten plums or rotten apricots or rotten gooseberries?

Omar I think maybe . . .

Charlie I'd say plums.

Daniel *approaches.*

Daniel Care for some sand?

He pours a handful of sand over **Omar***'s sandwich.*

Omar Oh.

Daniel I thought it would make it tastier!

He goes back to his own lunch.

Omar My mouth was really looking forward to eating that, Charlie.

Charlie I know.

Omar I was really hungry and that sandwich had last night's left-over chicken, which was really tasty.

We see H20 appear, slowly approaching **Daniel**. *Only* **Omar** *can see this.*

Charlie You can share mine if you want?

Omar *watches H20 blowing steam all over* **Daniel**.

Charlie And you can have my yoghurt. It's plum flavoured.

Omar *still distracted.*

Charlie Omar?

Omar Yeah?

H20 disappears.

Charlie You can have this.

Omar Oh.

He takes the yoghurt.

Omar (*shouting over*) Thanks, Daniel! Now I truly have a *sand-wich*!

Laughter from other kids.

Daniel *stands up and glares at* **Omar**.

Charlie I'm not sure it was a good thing to say that, Omar.

Omar I don't either.

Charlie Being smart with a bully isn't very smart.

Omar I know.

Charlie Daniel's clenching his teeth and looks quite angry.

Omar He looks a bit like a rottweiler.

Charlie I'm getting a little bit frightened. Can you tell me that protection prayer again please?

Omar It's . . .

Suddenly, **Daniel** *charges, launching his head towards* **Omar***'s stomach, growling.* **Omar** *throws himself onto the floor to dodge him and* **Daniel** *falls over the empty chair.*

Mrs Hutchinson Daniel! What are you doing?!

Daniel *stands and straightens himself out.*

Daniel Sorry, Mrs Hutchinson.

Mrs Hutchinson Follow me, now.

Mrs Hutchinson *leads.*

Daniel *follows, but stops by* **Omar**.

Daniel Don't think I don't know the worst thing about you. You're Muslim. All your mums look like letterboxes and bank robbers . . . I saw *your* mum the other day . . . in black . . . looking like a bank robber. You better go back to your own country before they kick you all out.

Mrs Hutchinson (*off-stage*) Daniel!

Daniel Coming, Mrs Hutchinson!

He exits.

Omar How could anyone think my mum looks like a bank robber?

Charlie I've met her and I don't think she does.

Omar Daniel is stupid not to tell the difference.

Charlie Bank robbers steal.

Omar My mum would never steal.

Charlie Bank robbers have poisonous warts.

Omar My mum only has one wart and it's not poisonous.

Charlie Bank robbers have bad breath cos they don't brush their teeth.

Omar My mum brushes her teeth twice a day and her breath is minty fresh.

Charlie Bank robbers scrunch up their face like this (*demonstrates*).

Omar My mum smiles.

Charlie Bank robbers are ugly, due to bad thoughts.

Omar My mum is beautiful, due to lovely thoughts.

Charlie I'd say a bank robber is a lot different to your mum.

Omar I would too. What did he mean . . . 'before they kick us all out?'

Charlie I don't know. I know about bank robbers. But I don't know about that. Ask your mum?

Omar No I don't want to tell Mum or Dad. They get all stressy and worried and make a big fuss . . . and that would definitely make Daniel worse.

Charlie Tell Maryam?

Omar Maybe. She might be annoying, but she used to stand up for me when I was little and went to the same school.

Charlie Yeah, tell Maryam.

Omar But then again, she is a huge snitch these days. The other day she snitched on me for stealing the batteries in the remote and I was banned from video games. No, I can't trust her.

Charlie Who can you trust?

Omar Reza!

Scene Nine

Omar (*to audience*) My cousin Reza . . . I could trust him! Luckily we were travelling up to Leeds that weekend in the Peanut.

Dad Get in the Peanut everyone! Everyone to the Peanut!

Omar The 'Peanut' is Dad's car . . . cos his number plate is . . . PE14NUT . . . Peanut!

They're all on the motorway now.

Omar Is this the M25, Dad?

Dad No it's the M1.

Omar Can we go on the M40?

Dad I'm afraid we have to stay on the M1.

Omar But I like the M40!

Esa Pee pee!

Mum Did you say you need to pee, Esa?

Esa Pee pee!

Mum I knew I shouldn't have given him that apple juice.

Dad Can you hold it until we get to the next service station, Esa?

Esa Pee pee, big pee pee!

Mum How long till the next service station?

Dad Six miles.

Mum He's only little, he can't hold it that long.

Maryam We should have put a nappy on him, Mum!

Omar Can you make sure you don't pee on me, Esa?

Maryam He better not do it on me!

Omar Or me!

Mum Stop it, you lot!

Dad Alright. Let's stop on the hard shoulder.

Omar Why is it called the 'hard shoulder'?

Dad I don't know.

Omar Why is it called the 'hard shoulder', Mum?

Mum I don't know, Omar!

Omar Is there a 'soft shoulder'?

Esa Pee pee spray spray!

Mum No, Esa, wait!

Omar Luckily, we managed to stop in time.

Then . . . six days later . . . well, that's how it felt . . . we got to Reza's.

We are now at **Reza***'s house in Leeds.* **Reza** *is fixing his bike.*

Omar How old are you now, Reza?

Reza Twelve.

Omar Wow.

Reza Next year I'll be thirteen. A proper teenager.

Omar That's super-cool.

Reza Pass me that spanner there, bro.

Omar *passes it to him.*

Omar I didn't know you could fix bikes.

Reza I can fix cars as well.

Omar Can you?

Reza I topped up the oil in Mum's banger.

Omar That's even cooler.

Reza I know.

Omar How did you manage to get so many toys?

Reza I just ask Mum and Dad.

Omar It never works for me.

Reza You need to ask a minimum of twenty-seven times.

Omar I knew you must have great pester-power skills. Reza?

Reza Yeah?

Omar This boy at school called Daniel said soon . . . 'they were going to kick us all out' . . . 'all the Muslims' . . . are they gonna?

Reza That's right.

Omar What?!

Reza That Daniel's right. All the Muslims are probably gonna be kicked out of the country soon . . . and then we'll probably have World War Three, bro.

Omar World War Three?!

Reza Yep. We'll all have to live in Pakistan.

Omar Have you ever been to Pakistan?

Reza Once, when I was five.

Omar What's it like? Will we like living there?

Reza Well the pizza is yuck . . . and you can hardly understand what people are saying.

Omar Why?

Reza Cos they speak in Urdu. You can't speak Urdu, can you?

Omar No.

Reza Well, then, you won't understand what they're saying.

Omar Can Charlie come?

Reza Who's Charlie? Is he Muslim?

Omar No.

Reza Then no, he can't.

Omar I don't want to go to Pakistan.

Reza Me neither. But it's gonna happen. This spanner's rubbish . . . hang on.

He exits.

Omar I couldn't sleep that night. Or on Saturday night. Or on the motorway home. Kept thinking about the day when they might 'kick us all out' . . . and the other stuff Daniel said about 'letterboxes' and 'bank robbers'. And about Mrs Rodgers . . . and whether she wants to 'kick us all out' as well?!

And then I started thinking about what I should do? Shall I tell Mum about what Daniel said? What Reza said? Shall I start learning Taekwondo? Judo? Maybe I need to get tough so I can protect my little brother? Yeah! Maybe that's what I've gotta do. Get tough. Fight back. Be nasty back. Kick *them* out. Yes! Kick *them* out! Mrs Rodgers first! Cos she's upset Mum real bad. Yes! I'll start with Mrs Rodgers.

Finally . . . we reached home and . . .

Suddenly, we hear the sound of a siren.

Omar (*to audience*) Oh no! They're coming to 'kick us out'!

Maryam What's that, Mum?!

Omar Is that a police car?!

Dad It's an ambulance!

Maryam What's an ambulance doing on our road?

Mum Gosh.

Omar The lights are flashing like crazy!

Maryam Paramedics.

Omar Para-what?

Maryam There's paramedics coming out.

Omar Are they like doctors?

Mum I wonder who it's for.

Maryam They're walking towards our house.

Omar It can't be for us.

Maryam Well, they're walking towards it.

Omar Nope. They're going next door.

Maryam Oh yeah.

Beat.

Realising at precisely the same time.

Everyone It's Mrs Rodgers!

Blackout.

End of Act One.

Interval.

Act Two

Scene One

Lights up.

As we left off.

Omar Oh no! Something must have happened to Mrs Rodgers!

Mum I should go! Check if she's ok!

Maryam No way, Mum!

Omar It's all my fault!

Maryam She's horrible, no way!

Omar For thinking nasty thoughts!

Mum Omar, hush!

Omar All the para-whats-its are going into Mrs Rodgers' house!

Mum I should go. Should I go?

Dad Yes, go.

Mum What if she doesn't want me there? What if she sends me away and shouts at me in front of everyone?

Maryam That's exactly what she'll do, Mum!

Dad It doesn't matter, darling. You go. At least you'll have done the right thing. Go.

Maryam She doesn't deserve it!

Mum Right. I'm going.

She exits.

We are now outside.

A paramedic wheels **Mrs Rodgers** *out on a trolley.*

Mum Mrs Rodgers! Are you ok?

Trolley pauses.

Mrs Rodgers *doesn't respond.*

Mum I'm here with you. I mean, if you want.

She puts her hand out. **Mrs Rodgers** *takes hold of it.*

Mrs Rodgers John isn't here.

Mum I am.

A pause.

Mrs Rodgers *stares at* **Mum**.

Mrs Rodgers I slipped.

Mum Don't worry. I'm here with you. Everything's gonna be ok.

Mrs Rodgers *is wheeled off.*

Scene Two

Montage.

Dad Have you checked in on Mrs Rodgers?

Esa Rodgers . . . Rodgers!

Mum Does Mrs Rodgers need anything from the supermarket?

Esa Rodgers . . . Rodgers!

Dad Should Omar pop over and check Mrs Rodgers' TV is working properly?

Esa Rodgers . . . Rodgers!

Mum Should Esa pick some flowers from the garden to cheer Mrs Rodgers up?

Esa Rodgers . . . Rodgers!

Omar (*to audience*) All we seemed to talk about in our house for the next little while was how Mrs Rodgers was doing. Dad?

Dad Yes?

Omar You know Mrs Rodgers is now a totally different person?

Dad Yes?

Omar Like, she isn't weird and mean anymore . . . and instead she's super-happy?

Dad Yes?

Omar Could it be because the fall made her brain work differently?

Dad *and* **Mum** *laugh.*

Dad Although that is possible . . . I think it had more to do with what she might have been reading before . . . or listening to . . . or watching.

Omar What?

Dad It's hard to explain, son . . . you're too young . . . but sometimes . . . people might receive wrong information about something . . . what they might have heard about Muslim people. Whereas now, she knows what we're actually like. Because she's met us. Maybe she'd never met a Muslim family before. We should invite her to our house during Ramadan . . . what d'you think, Aisha?

Mum I think that's a lovely idea.

Omar Won't that be a bit awkward?

Mum Why?

Omar Because we'll be fasting? You can't eat or drink?

Dad At Iftar. Sunset. When we can eat. We can invite her for our Iftar meal.

Mum She'll love it.

Esa Rodgers . . . Rodgers!

Scene Three

School bell.

In the classroom.

Charlie So, wait, Omar . . . in Ramadan . . . you can't eat or drink for a whole month?

Omar *laughs.*

Charlie Not even water?!

Omar *laughs.*

Charlie Won't people die if they do that?

Omar *continues laughing.*

Charlie Why y'laughing?

Omar *carries on laughing.*

Charlie It's a serious thing!

Omar You only have to stop eating when the sun is out. All other times, you can eat what you want, and you can eat lots, so you stay alive.

Charlie Phew. But why do people do it?

Omar Well my Qur'an teacher . . . Auntie Amal . . . she's not really my auntie . . . but we call all ladies my mum's age 'auntie' . . . she said . . . you learn to appreciate what you have . . . cos some people in the world don't have anything. And also, for a whole month, you get extra reward points from Allah. Seventy times more!

Charlie I'd like to get those points. Is it hard?

Omar Yeah.

Charlie Oh.

Omar But you have the Eid feast to look forward to at the end of the month!

Charlie One month is a lot of time.

Omar It is. But the devil is locked up during Ramadan /

Charlie Devil?!

Omar So he can't persuade us to eat when our tummies are rumbling.

Charlie What does this devil look like?

Omar Like this. (*He embodies a devil.*)

He starts creeping towards **Charlie**.

Charlie Oh no, Omar. That's scary.

Charlie *freaking out and avoiding* **Omar**.

Omar A nasty creature counting down the days to Ramadan . . . cos he knew he was gonna get locked away.

Charlie Would the devil get you? Kidnap you?

Omar Maybe! (*Grabs* **Charlie**.) And then he whispers to you to do bad things.

Charlie Like what?

Omar Like 'go and eat your sister's hidden stash of chocolate'. Which I did, once. (*Lets* **Charlie** *go.*) But it's ok . . . cos on the Night of Power I'm planning on asking Allah for a lifetime supply of chocolate of my own.

Charlie What's the 'Night of Power'?

Omar It's in the last ten days of Ramadan . . . and you can get the same reward points in one night, that it would take one thousand months to get!

Charlie Wow.

Omar And all the angels come down to Earth and you can ask Allah for anything you want.

Charlie Like a Kia Sportage GT-Line S 1.6 Hybrid or something?!

Omar Oh my gosh, Charlie! I want a Kia Sportage GT-Line S 1.6 Hybrid!

Mrs Hutchinson *enters.*

Mrs Hutchinson Happy Ramadan, Omar!

Omar Thank you, Mrs Hutchinson.

Mrs Hutchinson Are you fasting?

Omar No, I'm not allowed.

Mrs Hutchinson Oh, well. I'm happy to go easy on you in PE if you ever do.

Mrs Hutchinson *exits.*

Charlie Daniel's looking.

Omar I know.

Charlie He looks a bit red . . . and fidgety . . . and really cross.

Omar I know.

Charlie It would be really lovely if you weren't a 'trouble magnet' today, Omar.

Omar He's coming over!

Charlie Oh no.

Daniel *approaches.*

Daniel You're a teacher's pet!

He smudges **Omar***'s chalk drawing.*

Omar Daniel!

Daniel Oops!

Omar (*to* **Daniel**) Go away, Daniel.

Daniel What will you do? Call your girlfriend, Mrs Hutchinson?

Charlie She's not his girlfriend, ok?

Daniel (*to* **Omar**) Have you got your suitcase packed?

Omar No, why?

Daniel For when they kick you out?

Omar Leave me alone.

Daniel Bet your mum's well rich.

Charlie Why?

Daniel Robbing all those banks.

Mrs Hutchinson Everything ok over there?

Daniel Yes, Mrs Hutchinson.

He leaves.

Charlie Maybe I shouldn't have said that!

Omar He's so mean.

Charlie He's making me feel shaky and sick.

Omar Me as well.

Charlie *exits.*

H20 appears.

Music.

Omar *clings to him.*

Needing comfort from him.

A few seconds.

Scene Four

The sound of the call to prayer. Dinner table.

Mrs Rodgers Where's the mini one?

Omar Sleeping.

Mum Would you like more rice, Mrs Rodgers?

Mrs Rodgers I think I might have another samosa.

Mum There you go.

Mrs Rodgers Thank you.

Mum Maryam, slow down.

Omar She's starving!

Mrs Rodgers I see.

Omar Normally she eats the same amount as me, but now she's eating like a bear who's been hibernating.

Maryam Shut it, Omar.

Omar Yesterday, Mum had to stop her eating all the samosas.

Dad She needs the energy . . . she's got another science test in the morning.

Mum And she'll do much better this time.

Maryam I better do better!

Omar She's angry, Mrs Rodgers . . . cos last time she only got a C.

Maryam Shut it, Omar.

Omar We're a sciencey family, Mrs Rodgers so /

Mum Hush, Omar.

Dad She's prepared a lot harder this time /

Mum And you've gone through a lot of changes recently /

Maryam Changes?! Can you just stop it please!

Dad We're not upset with you, Maryam /

Mum We know you can do better /

Maryam Well, it's not my fault is it? You're the ones who made me move to this stupid school!

Mum Maryam!

Maryam I'm going!

Mum Maryam!

Awkward silence.

Mum Sorry about that, Mrs Rodgers.

Mrs Rodgers That's quite alright.

Mum She's being very hard on herself. (*Changing the subject.*) Omar's been very good today . . . setting out the table for Iftar!

Omar Yes . . . and I took all the stones out of the dates and put nuts in instead.

Mrs Rodgers They were scrumptious.

Omar Why are they called stones?

Dad They're actually seeds.

Omar If it was a real stone you'd smash your teeth!

Mrs Rodgers Quite right.

Omar Or if you managed to swallow it . . . it would stay in your tummy forever!

Mrs Rodgers Yes.

Omar And you'd have to poop it out! A big fat slodgy smelly /

Dad Shall we talk about something else, Omar?

Mum Anyway, Omar set the table really neatly, like in a restaurant.

Omar But Mum said not to use the fancy glasses.

Mrs Rodgers I don't need fancy.

Mum I just didn't want you to break them, Omar. Otherwise I have no problem using them, Mrs Rodgers.

Omar Dad, can I eat another chocolate from the box Mrs Rodgers brought?

Dad Actually I realised . . . they contain alcohol. It says on the box. So sadly, we can't eat them.

Omar Orrrr . . . they were so nice!

Mrs Rodgers I'm sorry about that.

Dad No problem at all . . . it's the thought that counts!

Mum That's right!

Omar You can't eat the thought.

Dad Omar! (*To* **Mrs Rodgers**.) Maybe you can take them with you . . . and enjoy them yourself?

Mrs Rodgers (*taking them*) I'm never one to say no to chocolate!

Omar Oh no!

Everyone What?

Omar Am I going to be drunk now?!

Mrs Rodgers *finds this hysterical. Then her phone rings.*

Mrs Rodgers Oooh. Phone. (*Answering.*) John! I can't talk right now . . . I'm eating Ramadan dinner with the Muslims . . . yes it was, John . . . they put less chilli in their food for me . . . it was delicious, John!

Omar (*to audience*) Mrs Rodgers came over every day for Iftar. I went to get her from her house. It was only twelve steps from her front door to ours, which takes me about twelve seconds. But it takes Mrs Rodgers sixty seconds. I timed it. It wasn't long before she got used to the Iftar routine . . .

Mrs Rodgers There's only one minute left! Put the Islam Channel on! Or we'll miss that nice song that tells you when to break your fast!

Esa *comes in and joins them.*

Omar The 'Adhaan'?

Mrs Rodgers Yes! The 'Adhaan'! Ready, Esa?

Esa Ready . . . ready!

Mrs Rodgers Five!

Esa Five!

Mrs Rodgers Four!

Esa Four!

Mrs Rodgers Three!

Esa Three!

Mrs Rodgers Two!

Esa Two!

Mrs Rodgers One!

Esa One!

Mrs Rodgers It's dinner time! Get the dates!

Esa Get the dates!

Scene Five

Night.

Alarm clock.

Maryam Get up, brat face.

Omar What time is it?!

Maryam 2 a.m.

Omar (*to audience*) I made it. To the weekend, without getting my bones broken by Daniel. And I was going to be fasting! Which meant . . . one step closer to my Kia Sportage GT-Line S 1.6 Hybrid. Mum and Dad said 'no' to fasting at first . . . but I turned up the turbo on my pester power!

He runs to the kitchen table.

Midnight feeeeaaaast!

Dad How are you this perky, this early in the morning?

Omar You sound different, Dad!

Dad Do I?

Omar And look different!

Dad Really?

Omar You as well, Mum.

Mum Ok.

Omar Like half-zombies.

Mum Ha, ha.

Omar You're all slow and slurry like there's thick zombie slime everywhere.

Mum Eggs?

Omar You see, usually you would have said 'would you like some eggs?' . . . but now it's just . . . 'eggs?'

Dad H-hot.

Omar You would have said 'be careful, it's hot'.

Dad Just be careful. Kettle. Hot.

Omar 'Kettle. Hot.' (*Laughs.*) Adults are funny. I can't understand why they have different levels of energy depending on how much sleep or coffee they've had.

Maryam Can you do less talking please?

Omar I'm basically the same all the time.

Dad I've realised.

Omar Maryam . . . you're at least quarter zombie . . . which means you're on your way to being an adult.

Maryam Less talking. Less.

Omar (*to audience*) I was forced to have some egg. And porridge. With biscuit spread. Then back to bed for more sleep until I woke up again at 8 a.m. I just had to remember not to eat breakfast and not to drink anything. It was easy! I wasn't hungry or thirsty at all.

The sound of a clock ticking.

9 a.m.

This is so easy!

10 a.m.

Going great!

11 a.m.

No problem at all!

12 . . .

We hear a loud tummy rumble.

Omar Ok, distraction. Build Lego triceratops! Or a Lego T-Rex? Or a Lego /

Dad Come on, Omar . . . get in the Peanut!

Omar (*to audience*) We were off to the supermarket. Which did not help things.

We see large theatrical versions of the following foods floating around **Omar** *and looking delicious.*

Omar Pain au chocolat. Waffles. Crumpets. Even things I don't like . . . like quiche. Looking yummier than I had ever seen quiche look before!

We hear another tummy grumble.

Omar Dad?

Dad Yes?

Omar I really really really want a pain au chocolat.

Dad Now?

Omar Yes.

Dad You want to break your fast?

Omar Can I?

Dad Of course.

Omar But are you sure Allah won't mind?

Dad Allah will just be happy that you wanted to try in the first place.

Omar Are you sure?

Dad There's a reason kids don't have to fast.

Omar Thanks, Dad.

He runs towards and hugs the giant pain au chocolat.

(*To audience.*) For the record . . . I tried again next weekend and kept the whole fast.

Scene Six

School bell.

The classroom.

Mrs Hutchinson Does anyone know what 'DNA' is?

Omar (*to audience*) I know! But I can't put my hand up cos Daniel will get mad.

Mrs Hutchinson 'DNA'? Anyone? Anyone heard that before?

Nobody answers.

Mrs Hutchinson No one? Ok. Does anyone know what genes are?

Omar (*to audience*) I know!

Laura*'s hand goes up.*

Mrs Hutchinson Yes, Laura?

Laura Clothes.

James*'s hand goes up.*

Mrs Hutchinson No. James?

James Genies?

Mrs Hutchinson Not genies, no.

Omar (*to audience*) It was unbearable! I couldn't take it anymore! (*To* **Mrs Hutchinson**.) I know!

Mrs Hutchinson Yes, Omar?

Omar Genes are what make us what we are. They're like special instructions. They decide what colour our eyes are . . . and things like that. And DNA is where the genes are found. Lots of them!

Mrs Hutchinson Well . . . I'm astonished. Where did you learn that?

Omar My parents are both scientists. It's kind of their favourite topic.

Charlie *gives* **Omar** *a high-five.*

Mrs Hutchinson Well, I'm very impressed . . . and you are absolutely correct. Did everyone hear that?

Omar (*to audience*) I'm pretty sure Daniel did. And I'm pretty sure he's glaring at me.

Charlie Daniel's looking.

Omar I know.

Mrs Hutchinson Did everyone hear?

All Yes, Mrs Hutchinson.

Mrs Hutchinson And we're going to learn more about DNA and genes . . . and many more amazing science facts on our trip to the Science Museum! Come on, let's go!

They all begin to exit.

Daniel *walks past staring at* **Omar**.

Omar Every time I saw him, I kept thinking about what he said . . . that I would be kicked out of my home and sent to a country I'd never visited. And Reza telling me it was all true.

Outside the school gates. Busy traffic in the background.

Mrs Hutchinson Ok, everyone. I hope you're all as excited as I am about our visit this morning. But I want listening ears on the ready. I want everybody paying attention at all times. Ok?

All Yes, Mrs Hutchinson.

Mrs Hutchinson We're going to split you up into six groups. We've got three teaching assistants . . . and three generous parents. Who are going to look after a group each.

Omar I could tell Mrs Hutchinson was a bit stressed . . . cos some of her curls were sticking out in funny directions . . . completely ignoring gravity.

Mrs Hutchinson So listen carefully. I'm going to read out who's in which group . . .

Omar (*to audience*) Please don't put me in Daniel's group. I even have my fingers crossed . . . look. I know I'm not supposed to believe in crossing fingers . . . but I need to try everything!

Mrs Hutchinson . . . Laura . . . Daniel . . . and Omar.

Omar (*to audience*) Noooo!

Mrs Hutchinson Ok. If you could all go and stand by Mrs Lishmund.

Omar (*to audience*) And Charlie was put in a whole different group!

Omar *and* **Daniel** *stand by each other.*

Mrs Hutchinson Ok, now that we're all in our groups . . . let's start walking to the Underground station!

They set off.

Daniel *grabs* **Omar** *and pulls him back.*

Daniel Your girlfriend Charlie can't save you now.

Omar *laughs.*

Omar (*to audience*) Why was I laughing?! I'm in a horrible situation! Why am I laughing?! I'm about to get hit by the worst bully in the world!

Daniel *grabs* **Omar** *by his jumper.*

Daniel Oh, so you think it's funny do you, teacher's pet?!

Omar *just stares.*

Daniel Do you?!

Omar *stares.*

Daniel I said, 'do you'?!

Omar Our group. The class. They've gone.

Daniel *releases him.*

Daniel What?

Omar Everyone's gone.

Daniel No.

Omar I think we've been left behind.

All of a sudden **Daniel** *starts wailing like a baby.*

Daniel Waaaaaa! We're lost! We're gonna die!

Omar Erm. Don't worry. Daniel. Erm. I've been on the Underground lots of times with my mum and dad.

Daniel *continues wailing.*

Omar But it does look a little bigger now. And darker. And noisier. Scarier.

He sniffs.

And it smells of wee.

Daniel (*crying*) Oh no, I've done a wee in my trousers!

Omar Oops. Ok, let's not panic. Even though I am, a bit. Let's think. Erm . . .

A train rumbles past onto the platform.

Omar Let's jump on!

Daniel What if it's the wrong train?!

Omar My instinct is telling me to jump on. Come on!

He grabs **Daniel***'s hand and they jump on.*

Daniel What's instinct?

Omar It's like . . . like . . . with animals . . . with sea turtles . . . when the babies hatch . . . and they move towards the ocean without anybody telling them which way to go. Or when baby kangaroos jump into their mummy's pouch.

Daniel Oh.

Omar *is still holding* **Daniel***'s hand.*

Daniel Don't let go, Omar.

Omar I won't. (*To audience.*) Ok, Omar, now is not the time to think about when Daniel picked his nose earlier. (*To* **Daniel**.) We're going to South Kensington Station, right?

Daniel I don't know.

Omar I remember Mrs Hutchinson saying that. And I remember when I went to the museum with Mum and Dad . . . and we had to walk through a long tunnel.

Daniel So do you know where to go?

Omar Yes. Look on that map up there. See if you can find South Kensington on it.

They search.

Daniel (*sobbing*) I can't find it!

Omar Ok. I think we have to change trains again.

Daniel *sobs.*

Daniel Let's tell someone we're lost!

Omar No. We're not lost. (*To audience.*) We were.

Daniel Let's tell someone! That woman over there on her phone! Or that man next to her on his phone! Or the man opposite on his phone! Or anyone of the grown-ups around us on their phones!

Omar Don't panic. We're gonna be fine. My instinct is now telling me to get off at the next stop.

Announcement This is Baker Street.

Omar I know Baker Street. I'm sure I've been here before.

Daniel Do you think Mrs Hutchinson knows we're lost?

Omar I imagine her hair is going a bit crazy. Come on, there's the exit.

Daniel Are we not getting another train?

Omar No. Let's exit. Come!

They come out of the station. Noise of a busy road.

Daniel I don't know this road.

Omar I'm sure I do. I remember all these cafes . . . and the Sherlock Holmes Museum. Mum and Dad's favourite. Now . . . let me think . . .

A **Homeless Man** *dressed in rags puts his hand on* **Omar***'s shoulder. We can't clearly see his face.*

They scream.

Omar/Daniel Aaaaaaahhhhhh!

Daniel *and* **Omar** *run through a busy high street.*

We hear a few voices from strangers: 'Hey, watch where you're going!', 'Are you kids ok?', etc.

When it's safe, they come to rest. **Daniel** *wails.*

Daniel What was that?!

Omar I've never seen anything like that before!

Daniel It was a monster!

Omar It was like a zombie.

Daniel It didn't even have a proper face!

Omar This is when I could definitely use H20's help.

Daniel Who's H20?!

Omar No one.

Daniel Let's ask H20 for help?!

Omar Look, Daniel /

Daniel Ask H20 for help!

Omar Daniel /

Daniel (*calling*) H20! H20! Help!

Omar Daniel! It's gonna be ok. (*To audience.*) That was a lie. But it's what grown-ups would say. Grown-ups! (*To* **Daniel**.) Daniel, what would your parents do if they were lost?

Daniel They would look for the way on their phones.

Omar Right. We don't have phones.

Daniel What would yours do? If they were in trouble and they were going to die like us?

Omar Well, anytime there's a big problem, my parents ask Allah for help. That's one thing they always tell me a lot. To ask Allah for everything.

Daniel And did you?

Omar Erm. Actually no. I forgot.

Daniel Ask him!

Omar Ok.

Daniel Ask him! Ask Allah!

Omar (*to audience*) I didn't know the exact Arabic prayer for being lost with a bully and being chased by a zombie, but Dad said that Allah knows all languages and we can speak to him however we need to.

Daniel Ask Allah!

Omar Ok.

He closes his eyes and starts whispering. After a few seconds **Omar** *opens his eyes.* **Daniel** *is staring right at him.*

Daniel Well? Did you ask him? Is he gonna help us?

Omar Of course he will . . . Allah always helps.

Daniel But do you think he heard you? You were whispering so quiet. I couldn't even hear you . . . and I'm right next to you.

Omar Yes, he did. It's God! God can hear everything . . . even whispers. Even when you talk in your head.

Daniel But what did you say?

Omar I said . . . 'Allah, I'm sorry I forgot to ask you before, but we're kind of lost and we need your help. We lost all our teachers and we don't know where they are. We don't even know where we are actually. And also, there might be a zombie trying to catch us. I'm trying to look after Daniel, as he's very worried and crying' /

Daniel I'm not crying /

Omar 'Please can you help us, Allah? I don't know how, but I guess you know.' Something like that.

Daniel Oh, ok.

Omar Don't worry, you'll get back home to your mum and dad.

Daniel If they even notice I'm gone.

Omar What?

Daniel If they even care.

Omar Of course they care. That's what parents do. I think you're a bit hard to miss. I mean, if you weren't there, I would notice.

Daniel Really?

Omar Super-definitely.

Daniel Yes. But . . . my parents . . . all they care about is my little sister. Cos she's always in hospital.

Omar Oh. Is she . . . is she gonna be ok?

Daniel I don't know . . . she's always sick and having operations.

He starts crying again.

And I do care about her . . . I do . . . I do . . . but what about me? I might as well not be there. I just get in the way when they need to look after her.

Omar *moves closer to* **Daniel**.

Omar I don't know what I would do if that happened to me. Yeah. That must be pretty tough.

Daniel *sniffs, wipes his tears.*

Daniel So, what now? Do we just sit here?

Omar I don't think so. The zombie might find us.

Daniel What then?

Omar Let's walk.

Daniel Ok.

They start walking.

It's quieter.

Less traffic, sounds of birds and Regent's Park.

Omar Daniel was a bit calmer now. I was kind of proud of him. Even though he still smelt of wee. We walked and walked and then . . . (*To* **Daniel**.) I know why this place is so familiar!

Daniel What?

Omar London Central Mosque! That's where I had my first halal sweets. That's where a man gave me ten pounds, just for being cute! That's where I prayed with my mum!

The **Homeless Man** *approaches again.*

Omar Zombie!

Daniel Aaarrrggghhh!

Omar Run to the mosque!

They make a sprint for it, run and run, until they bump into a woman at the mosque.

Mosque Woman Hey, hey, hey . . . is everything ok?!

Omar We're lost! We were on a school trip and got lost! And tried to find the Science Museum but we were lost!

Daniel And we asked Allah for help! And then we got chased by a zombie! A zombie!

Mosque Woman It's ok . . . you're safe. Where is this 'zombie', my child?

Daniel There!

Homeless Man *approaches.*

Omar He's there!

Mosque Woman My dears, that's no 'zombie'.

Homeless Man Everything alright?

Mosque Woman Yes, all ok.

Homeless Man They looked lost . . . I thought they'd lost their parents or summin'.

Mosque Woman Thank you. Here. take this.

She give the **Homeless Man** *a tenner.*

Homeless Man Oh thanks, maam. God bless. See ya.

Omar Bye.

Homeless Man Bye little'ens.

Omar (*to* **Mosque Woman**) What's his name?

Mosque Woman Ask him.

Omar What's your name?

Homeless Man Name's Eddy.

Daniel Eddy?

Homeless Man That's right. I would've been able to catch up with you if it wasn't for my bad knee! Ha! Anyway . . . see ya!

Homeless Man *exits.*

Mosque Woman Looks like he was trying to help you.

Omar Feel stupid now.

Mosque Woman Right. Why don't you tell me which school you're at. And I'll give them a ring.

Omar (*to audience*) We also got some juice and halal sweets.

Daniel Yum-mie!

Omar (*to audience*) This made Daniel's day.

Daniel I thought 'halal' was something bad . . . but these sweets are tasty!

Omar It's nice to see you smiling.

Beat.

Daniel Sorry that I've been mean.

Omar That's ok.

Daniel You're a pretty cool friend.

Omar Friend?

Daniel Erm . . . if you want . . . to be?

Dad *rushes in.*

Dad Omar!

Omar Dad!

Dad So happy to see you! And you, Daniel! My gosh . . . we were going nuts with . . . especially *your* mum and dad, Daniel.

Daniel Really?

Dad Absolutely.

Omar We met a 'homeless not so zombie man'.

Dad Did you?

Daniel Called Eddy.

Omar At first we were scared . . . but he's actually friendly.

Dad Well, I'm so thankful we've found you both. Come on.

Omar Are we going to the Science Museum?

Dad I think we've all had enough adventures for one day.

Scene Seven

Omar (*to audience*) A few days later . . . Daniel and his mum came to our house for Iftar.

Daniel's Mum We want to know every single bit of detail about what happened.

Mum Yes! Once the pizzas are done . . . every detail.

Omar Ok.

Daniel's Mum I'm so thankful they're safe.

Mum Anything could have happened /

Daniel's Mum I keep touching him and hugging him . . . checking he's still here.

Daniel She's started giving me non-stop hugs and kisses.

Daniel's Mum And I'm so grateful to the mosque for helping them.

Daniel Omar asked Allah for help and it was only after that we were saved.

Mum Yes, Omar was telling me /

Daniel So it must have been Allah that did it.

Daniel's Mum I'd love to visit the mosque and thank them personally?

Mum You're welcome to come with us /

Omar We're going there on Eid!

Daniel's Mum I'd love that. When is Eid?

Omar In three days! If the moon comes out.

Mum The moon tells us when Ramadan is over.

Daniel's Mum How fascinating /

Omar And if the new moon can't be seen, it's basically not Eid for another day and it's so annoying.

Mum *laughs.*

Mum We just keep an extra fast that day instead /

Daniel's Mum Well, whenever it is. I would be most honoured to come with you and thank them.

Omar We should tell the prime minister the mosque helped us!

Mum Oh of course! Do you have his phone number?

Both mums start laughing.

Omar Then they won't 'kick us out'?!

Mum Kick who out?

Omar All the Muslims! If they know that the mosque has nice people there . . . they might not 'kick us out'!

Beat.

Mum Where did you get an idea like that?

Omar Erm. I heard it . . . somewhere . . . and I even asked Reza and he said we'll all have to live in Pakistan.

Beat.

Mum That is never going to happen . . . don't listen to anyone who tells you that.

Daniel's Mum How awful.

Mum Kids make things up all the time. Always come and tell me or Dad if you ever hear anything like that again, ok?

Omar Ok.

Mum So we can give you the facts. Ok?

Omar Ok.

Daniel It was me!

Daniel's Mum What?

Daniel I said it! I'm sorry, Omar!

Daniel's Mum What? Why . . . why on Earth would you ever say anything like that, Daniel?!

Daniel I . . . I heard Uncle Peter say it.

Daniel's Mum What?!

Daniel When he was talking with another grown-up.

Daniel's Mum Uncle Peter?

Daniel (*reluctantly*) Yes.

Daniel's Mum Well . . . I think we need to have a word with Uncle Peter then.

Daniel And he said one of our prime ministers said Muslim mums look like 'letterboxes and bank robbers' . . . so I just said it to Omar to make him feel bad.

Daniel's Mum (*appalled*) Oh my goodness.

Daniel But I'm sorry now!

Daniel's Mum (*to* **Mum**) I'm so, so sorry about this.

Daniel I'm so, so sorry, Omar.

Daniel's Mum I'm horrified. I'm . . . utterly horrified, I don't know what to . . .

A beat.

Mum Daniel . . . it was very good of you to own up to that and tell the truth. It must have been really hard.

Daniel's Mum Omar. I am very proud that you are Daniel's friend . . . and I wouldn't want you going anywhere.

Omar Thank you, Daniel's mum.

Scene Eight

School bell.

Playground.

Omar So we're going to start from the beginning. Ok?

Charlie/Daniel Ok.

Omar You have never met each other before. Ok?

Charlie/Daniel Ok.

Omar You have never seen each other before. Ok?

Charlie/Daniel Ok.

Omar Now after three, I want you to say 'hello' and become friends. Ok?

Charlie/Daniel Ok.

Omar I'm going to count you in. Ok?

Charlie/Daniel Ok.

Omar Three, two, one . . . go!

Awkward silence.

Daniel Hello.

Charlie Hello.

Daniel What's your name?

Charlie Charlie. What's your name?

Daniel Daniel.

Awkward silence.

Omar (*encouraging them*) And?

Charlie And . . . would you like to be my friend, Daniel?

Daniel I would love to be your friend, Charlie.

Charlie Would you like to play a game with me, Daniel?

Daniel I would love to play a game with you, Charlie.

Omar Excellent! (*To audience.*) It took a while . . . cos Charlie had never seen the nice version of Daniel. But I had been an accidental magnet and pulled them together. I was completely super-sure they'd get on. And I was right. We asked Daniel to play football with us in the playground, cos we realised nobody had even asked him before. It turned out he was better than anyone in the class at being goalie. And two days after . . . it was Eid . . . and . . .

We're at **Omar***'s house. Party music.*

Lots of background chatter. Colourful lights.

Omar Mum?!

Mum (*off-stage*) Yes?

Omar Are the brownies done?

Charlie Please be done!

Daniel Please, please, please.

Mum Almost.

Omar We're hungry, Mum!

Daniel Starving.

Omar Low battery mode.

Charlie 9 per cent.

Mum Have some grapes and cheese.

Omar We're hungry for brownies, Mum.

Daniel I like this song!

Mrs Rodgers *crosses, dancing and singing along with* **Esa**. *Completely lost in the music.*

Maybe it's bhangra – and **Mrs Rodgers** *knows all the Punjabi lyrics?*

Dad (*off-stage*) Reza's here!

Omar My cousin's here!

Reza (*enters*) Reza in da house!

Omar Reza!

Mum Reza?

Reza Eid Mubarak, Auntie!

Mum Eid Mubarak. Come in here for a sec.

Reza Why? Is it an Eid present or something?!

Mum I think we need to have a little word.

Reza About what, Auntie?

He leaves.

Omar Ooops. I think I know what that might be about.

Mrs Rodgers *crosses again, dancing and singing along with* **Esa**. *The boys happily join in. Maybe we see H20 as well – only* **Omar** *sees him.*

Dad *enters.*

Dad Where's Maryam gone?

Omar On the phone with her new best mate.

Dad Maryam! Come and have something to eat please.

Dad *leaves.*

Mum *enters.*

Mum Ok, the brownies are done!

Omar/Charlie/Daniel Yes!

Omar *takes the brownie tray off* **Mum**.

Omar (*to* **Daniel** *and* **Charlie**) Quick! Eat, before Esa comes and licks them all.

They scoff the brownies.

Sounds of the chocolate pleasure and brownie all over their faces. Mouths full.

Mum *enters holding* **Esa**, *covering his eyes so he can't see the brownies.*

Mum Slow down, boys!

Charlie They're so good, Omar's mummy!

Daniel Delicious!

Mum Don't tell Esa . . . he's got to have his lunch first.

As **Mum** *is leaving.*

Reza (*off-stage*) Thanks, Mrs Rodgers, but I really don't want to dance!

Mrs Rodgers Oh come on, young man, it's Eid!

She crosses again, this time dancing and singing along with an embarrassed and reluctant **Reza**, *who is being flung around.*

The boys laugh.

Reza (*as he whizzes past*) Stop laughing at me!

Reza *and* **Mrs Rodgers** *exit.*

Charlie Oh my gosh!

Daniel (*mouthful*) Hmnfwhat?

Charlie Your teeth are so brown!

They laugh.

Omar So are yours, Charlie!

They laugh more.

Daniel And yours, Omar!

Omar We've all got brown teeth!

Laughter continues.

The End.

www.ingramcontent.com/pod-product-compliance
Lightning Source LLC
LaVergne TN
LVHW052343100826
845147LV00021B/1162

* 9 7 8 1 3 5 0 6 4 2 0 4 1 *